RELATIONAL PRESENCE:
DECISION MAKING BEYOND CONSENSUS

by

Samuel G. Mahaffy

Copyright © 2012

by

Samuel George Mahaffy

All rights reserved. No part of this publication
may be reproduced, stored in a retrieval system
or transmitted in any form or by any means
electronic, mechanical, photocopying, recording,
or otherwise, without the prior written permission
of the author.

Author's dedication:

I dedicate this book to all the participants in decision making processes I have facilitated who have *shown up* to share the richness of their stories, their vision, their dreams, and their pain and sorrow. May the risks you take to speak from your heart and to speak truth to power deepen our search for relational wholeness.

OPEN JUNCTURE PUBLISHING CO.
624 W. Hastings. Ste. 5
Spokane, WA. 99218

Cover design and lay-out:
Laska Golden

Acknowledgement:

Reflective feedback from Dr. Renee Rinderknecht and Kari Joys, M.S. provided invaluable input in the preparation of this material.

Copyright © 2012

by

Samuel George Mahaffy

All rights reserved. No part of this publication may be reproduced, stored in a retrieval system or transmitted in any form or by any means electronic, mechanical, photocopying, recording, or otherwise, without the prior written permission of the author with the exception of brief quotations embodied in critical articles and reviews.

Recommendations

Samuel Mahaffy demonstrates a clear pathway for moving beyond 'winners' and 'losers' in decision making. The extraordinary gifts the author has in bringing conflicted parties together lay the groundwork for a new relational approach to decision making. This work is a 'must read' for facilitators, change agents, and anyone seeking to be an instrument of peace and reconciliation.

Kari Joys, M.S.
Founder & Director,
Center for Creative Change
Author: Choosing Light Heartedness
Public Speaker, Psychotherapist, Facilitator
www.kari-joys.com

Relational Presence brings forward an innovative and life-giving approach to decision making. It makes a significant contribution to research on heart intelligence. It is sure to be of value to anyone looking for an integral perspective on organizational development or facilitation of change.

Dr. Renee Rinderknecht
Founder, Center for Heart Presence
Author: Integral Pedagogy: Teaching with an
Open and Engaged Heart (Dissertation Research
at California Institute of Integral Studies)

The author invites your participation in the conversation about *relational presence*. Visit his website at www.samuelmahaffy.com. Send comments and feedback to: samuelmahaffy@gmail.com

Prologue

For most of my adult life, I have witnessed and participated in well-intentioned efforts under the banner of *consensus decision making* to make change processes more participatory, more inclusive, and more satisfying for participants. Yet, the way we make decisions in organizations in many ways remains broken. Ineffective decision making processes often reinforce power disparities and exclude those who most need to have a voice. Our best efforts at reaching consensus often leave one or more participants in decision making processes either empty or feeling that they have compromised their deepest held values. Is institutional decision making slowly killing our spirits? In the contemporary world there is a compelling need for decision making that transcends differences to find *shared higher purpose*. The achievement of our shared ideals and the very future of the planet may depend on it. Yet we collectively live with the negative outcomes of bad decisions still made by too few decision makers who put self-interest above the common good. Often democratic participation is a pretense that maintains the status quo. The near economic collapse of western economies and the crisis in access to food and health care around the world in this decade can be viewed from the perspective of decisions that have been made by too few participants holding too much power. Disparities in global access to life-sustaining resources mirror disparities in meaningful participation in decision making processes that may have life and death consequences. The rise of the *occupy movement* in the western world and the sweeping uprisings against totalitarianism around the world make sense when understood in terms of voices that have too long been silenced and ignored.

It was with great excitement that I discovered a fundamentally new approach for understanding decision making. While the name *relational constructionism* is a bit intimidating, the concept is simple. It prioritizes *relationship*. It breaks free from individualistic views of knowledge to understand that decision making is shaped in and through our social interdependence. This approach invites a more participatory approach to human engagement. Decision making is viewed as a communal construction or as *relational coordination*.

But my work on *Relational Presence* suggests that decision making may entail even more than *relational coordination*. I seek to articulate a fundamentally new view of decision making that builds on the *relational constructionist* perspective. The notion of *relational presence* as it unfolds in this work moves well beyond the framework of decision making processes where the majority rules and where there are 'winners' and 'losers.' I suggest that relational decision making be viewed as a sort of *mimetic movement* that compels participants to respond, to *move with,* to *mirror* each other. It is a dance of *self-discovery* and *other-discovery*. In this dance, might we go beyond *consensus decision making models* where participants simply agree to no longer disagree but never find *shared higher purpose*? I invite you to journey with me into this *quietly inviting* place of decision making where a *gathered community* meets with *attentiveness*, welcomes the *stranger* and in so doing welcomes new ideas and values *unknowing*. Relational presence has no agenda, because it is the agenda. The atmosphere of relational presence is thinner than the denseness of traditional decision making processes. It is the atmosphere of spirit, breath, renewal. Instead of focusing on the *turf* between *subject* and *object* in decision making, it focuses on the presence we feel when we are truly intimate with each other. I invite you to enter this exploration of *relational presence* in decision making with me.

Samuel G. Mahaffy

CONTENTS

1. Why Decision Making Needs a New Design

2. Decision Making for Efficiency

3. Decision Making Moves Away from a Problematizing Focus

4. The Great Promise of Consensus Decision Making

5. The Pitfalls of Consensus Decision Making

6. Finding our Way Forward: Beyond Consensus Decision Making

7. A Relational Constructionist Approach to Decision Making

8. Moving Beyond Relational Coordination in Decision Making

9. Accepting Disagreement and Differences

10. Discovering the Richness of Relationship in Decision Making

11. Discovering Relational Presence in Decision Making

12. Applying Relational Presence in Every Day Decision Making

Why Decision Making Needs a New Design

"There is a lie that must be named and a truth that must be told. Our institutions are killing our spirits. We are allowing it to happen. In exchange for an illusion of power and control, safety and security, we have betrayed our souls because we are afraid"

Diane Cory in
"The Killing Fields: Institutions and the Death of our Spirits"

The language of *separation,* of *confrontation,* of *division,* and of *duality* has largely shaped, during this century, the way we talk about decision making. The literature of organization development (OD) is filled with war and battle metaphors. "If you don't know who's with you and who's against you how do you know whom to welcome and whom to fear, or when to laugh and when to smile? If you don't know where the land mines are, every path must be a cautious one" (Weiss, 2003, p. 139). To design a decision making process in this context is to design a *battle plan.* In this depersonalization of both institutions and participants, decision making is not held in high esteem. It is necessary only to the extent that it is needed to efficiently accomplish some stated purpose. Power is prescribed to the decision makers at the top of a hierarchy.

The last decades have seen a revolt that calls for decision making to be more democratic and more *participatory.* Instead of seeking to have "rigorous opposition…fall into line (Weiss, 2003, p. 141) the emerging paradigm of modern OD has "emphasis on shared decision making, high levels of participation, and collaboration, human growth and fulfillment…" (Bartunek & Woodman, 2012, p. 732). In a context where decision making is increasingly global there is an imperative for practices that are more *collaborative* and *inclusive* if we are to survive and thrive on this planet. There is a clear need to "deepen awareness of the self, others, and the larger world" (Mirvis, 2010, p. 519) and to foster *dynamic relationships* (Stavros & Torres, 2008) that are "authentic" and "increase trust" (p. 82). In the "rapidly changing, turbulent, and uncertain environments" (Bolman & Deal, 2003, p. 67) in which organizations operate today, we must find new designs for decision making. It can no longer be left to organizational leaders in consultation with outside experts. Decision making is and must move down to "more local levels" (Senge, Kleiner, Roberts, Ross, Roth, & Smith, 1999, p. 18). In times of profound change, we must design decision making differently if we are to expect different outcomes.

David Cooperrider's (2012) highlighting of the critical importance of exploring deeper the *design* phase of Appreciative Inquiry (AI) is reflective of his sense that we must move from *reactive learning* from our mistakes in decision making processes to greater *anticipatory skills.* If we have *designed* decision making in a certain fashion, we can surely *re-design* it. If we are to move toward the "sacred potential of relational being" as Ken Gergen (2009, p. 388) suggests we must, we are compelled to discover in decision making processes *relational wholes* that transcend the individual differences that have divided us. We must move beyond the war and battle metaphors of decision making to uncover pathways to shared higher purpose.

The past decades have seen a plethora of approaches and methodologies developed to make decision making more participatory. The emphasis in decision making shifted from

Is there a better way?

"Occupy movements happen when people have lost their voice for too long. People are so beaten down by institutions and processes that have disenfranchised them, that there is nothing left to do but to rise up."

Michael Collier, Lay Pastor and Organizer Occupy Tacoma

"Then, are we all agreed?"

"We have been put in square boxes. Our power is gone and we are dying, for the power is not in us anymore."

From the words of Black Elk, a holy man of the Sioux Nation

increasing efficiency to methods described as *whole system change*. These include future search, open space, whole-scale change, and the conference model. The efforts to increase participation often emphasized *consensus decision making*. In its classical definition, consensus decision making seeks the unanimous agreement of participants on a particular decision or course of action (Herrera-Viedma, Herrera, & Chiclana, 2002). It seeks some balance between *maximum participation* and *maximum efficiency* (Hartnett, 2011). Yet even in its most recent iterations, experts on consensus decision making suggest that closure to such processes may well involve the group showing *empathy* for unsatisfied participants while moving ahead with ratification of the decision (Hartnett, 2011). Consensus decision making may have found some methods for achieving uneasy peace treaties without fundamentally changing the notion of decision making as a battle for turf. Clearly, a new *paradigm* with a new *design* may be needed.

The present work suggests that a re-design of decision making is not only possible, but essential. Building on the author's dissertation research on the *spatiality* of decision making through a relational constructionist lens (Mahaffy, 2012) this work searches for an approach to decision making that is more integral, more holistic, and more life-giving. It asks, *what is that place like where transformational change happens?* What is the place like, described by AI as the *positive life giving core* (Cooperrider & Sekerka, 2003) where "unions emerge" (Watkins & Stavros, 2010, p. 239) and "life-generating potentials merge" (p. 235)? This work seeks to take an uninhibited journey into the *mystery* of that place where the consciousness of *sacred presence* in human relationships and affairs is evident, where breakthrough decision making happens, and where groups find a *shared higher purpose*. In so doing, it seeks to articulate a way to make decision making processes more *life-giving*. It seeks to be a roadmap for a better way for facilitators, stakeholders, and decision makers. It seeks to support the *voice* of those who are too often excluded from decision making.

Decision Making for Efficiency

"Decision making in traditional organization development (OD) is purposeful toward increasing efficiency, increasing available resources for production, and maintaining power and control in an organizational context."

From Samuel Mahaffy
Relational Presence in Decision Making

Decision making, as an organizational field of practice, was born from and shaped by the drive for industrial efficiency (Watkins, 2010). The early model of organizational consulting was largely one of an expert who came into an organization to "tell and fix" (Bartunek & Woodman, 2012, p. 730). Decision making is not highly valued. It is useful and necessary only to the extent that it is required to fix some problem. "Decision making is viewed as an activity which absorbs the energy of those available, works on problems, and comes up with solutions which are determined in large measure by a random stream of events" (Pfeffer, 2005, p. 297). Sometimes described as the *garbage can model,* problems are fed into one end of a process with the hope that solutions will come out the other end. Consultants are experts who seek to make this process more efficient and enhance organizational purposes. Organizations in this view are "a social device for efficiently accomplishing through group means some stated purpose; it is the equivalent of the blueprint for the design of the machine which is to be created for some practical objective" (Katz & Kahn, 2005, p. 481).

These are the historic roots that still shape and color much of our decision making today in work places, universities, places of worship, and in community organizations. It is a hierarchical view where the task of senior managers, leaders, and facilitators is to manage resistance from the rank-and-file. Kanter (1988) writes that "the manager's first task is to *handle interference* or opposition that may jeopardize the project" (p. 191). 'Successful' meetings are those where the decisions made further the intended purposes of those in charge who called the meeting. They are meetings where many participants come 'on board' with a plan that has been shaped by a few. The literature of traditional OD is absorbed with the notion of *boundaries.* Boundaries may constrain who participates, what information is shared, what decisions can be made, and who will be assigned to implementation. They may keep out information and perspectives from both within and outside the group and the organization. Activities that cross or bridge established boundaries—*boundary spanning*—are viewed as problematic or a threat. Diversity of opinions and perspectives is something to be reduced and/or controlled.

The emphasis is on the *individual* as a performer or actor in the decision making process. Souder (1988) states a generalization that is frequently seen in traditional OD literature: "The generation of useful ideas depends largely on individual abilities" (p. 531). Groups are to be "properly constituted, structured, and guided" (p. 533) to minimize the risk of bad decisions. "Idea screening" (p. 535) may also be used to minimize the risk(s) of 'bad' decisions by controlling the information and perspectives that are brought before the decision making group. Decision making is focused on *solving a problem*, finding a solution, or making an organization

Responding to a Locust Plague: Impact of Decision Making on Absent Parties

Fields of grain surrounded the East African village of Senafe, Eritrea where I grew up. In the 1960's locust plagues sometimes descended on the fields, swarming into the valley like a thick, black, churning cloud. The locust swarms cut a clear swath through the grain fields, devouring what was anticipated to be the next grain crop that would sustain the villagers. In the life-cycle of the village this was an anticipated event. Villagers turned out with burlap sacks to throw over bushes, collecting bags full of locusts that would be roasted and stored. This tasty protein source replaced the lost grain crop and insured the survival of the village.

But in a meeting room, on another continent, the decision was made to send 'locust patrols' to help the Africans by eradicating the locusts. Tanker trucks pursued the locusts across Sub-Sahara Africa spraying the swarms with toxic chemicals. While their numbers were reduced, the locusts were not eradicated. The source of survival food for Eritrean villagers became poisoned.

The Eritrean villagers were the *absent voices* in the decision about how to fix their locust 'problem.' Their voice was not heard. The decision making process had life-and-death consequences that most affected those not invited into the conversation.

work better. The proposed 'solution' may not meet the needs of participants in the room, much less those whose *voices* have been disenfranchised and silenced.

Participants, affected by a decision, but not given *voice* in the decision making process, may be those most hurt. Such decision making processes tend to maintain power and control while presenting the illusion of participation.

Such are the roots of decision making in organizations today. While the last decades have seen efforts to move decision making to a new model, it is clear that the model designed for *efficiency* and for maintaining *power and control*, still holds a deep grip on how we make decisions even in progressive organizations.

Take a minute to reflect on a recent meeting you participated in that involved decision making. It may have been at work, in a university, or in a church. Reflect on that meeting. Ask yourself these questions:

➢ Who called the meeting and who controlled it? Who was in charge, and how did they maintain their position of being in charge?

➢ Who set the agenda for the meeting? Were participants involved in setting the agenda?

➢ Did you or others know what the likely outcome of the meeting would be before it started?

➢ Who was not in the room that should have been there? Were these people talked about? Were decisions made that obligated non-participants?

➢ Did you leave the meeting feeling heard? Were all voices in the room heard? Was there interrupting? Was there silence?

➢ What boundaries were set in the meeting—either visible or invisible? How did the meeting space affect the decisions that were made? Was there *gatekeeping* of information? Were there participants who were subtly or overtly excluded?

➢ Did the meeting deepen your relationship(s) with the other participants?

Are our decision making processes today still shaped by the *efficiency* paradigm?

Decision Making Moves Away from a Problematizing Focus

"Organization Development (in the modern context)...is a positive approach to organizational change with its emphasis on shared decision making, high levels of participation and collaboration, human growth and fulfillment..."

Bartunek & Woodman, 2012

Modern OD sees the evolution of "dialogic OD" and "turning away from diagnosis" (Bushe, 2010, p. 617). As happens in paradigm shifts (Kuhn, 1962) the practice of OD was gradually, but radically altered to such an extent that the field of practitioners would ask "why OD lives despite its pronounced death" (Bartunek & Woodman, 212, p. 727). But even modern OD carries skeletons from its past that included mechanistic and behavioristic approaches. The language of *diagnosis* is still very much alive in modern OD work. While continuing efforts are made to drive decision making models to be more participatory, there is still a view that is hierarchical. In the modern context, we turn to processes that are more participatory recognizing that *deep change* is more valuable than *quick fixes* (Nguyen Huy, 2012, p. 811). Modern OD is interested in "generative dynamics that lead to positive states or outcomes" (Stavros & Wooten, 2012, p. 826). Practitioners of AI involved in decision making processes have turned away from the "problematizing focus" (Cooperrider & Godwin, 21012, p. 740) of traditional OD and toward a focus on the "science and scholarship of the positive" (p. 741) and "innovation inspired by the best in life" (p. 743).

In this new context, *uncertainty* and *diversity* are no longer viewed as environmental instability that may be a potential threat. Instead, these present the opportunity for new ideas, new inputs and new organizational learning. Decision making contexts seek to create "a space for people who think differently, or come from different cultures and traditions, to work together to explore common ground that benefits them individually and benefits the organization or community" (Axelrod, Cady, & Holman, 2010, p. 371).

Decision making is now viewed—not as an individualistic and rationalistic mental process—but as a *transformative* process that grows out of a *relational*, social and cultural context. Understanding the complexities of decision making, the model moves toward a *relational* approach. In this new world the emphasis is on *dialogue*. Isaacs (1999) notes that "roots of the word *dialogue* come from the Greek words *dia* and *logos*. *Dia* means 'through'; *logos* translates to 'word,' or 'meaning.' In essence, a dialogue is a *flow of meaning*" (p. 18). Isaac understands *logos,* not in the sense of *law* or *rational word*, but rather in the more ancient and original meaning similar to the word *ligein,* in the sense of *gathering*. He notes that the word might best be translated into English as "relationship" (p. 19).

Relationship comes to take a much important role in decision making in the modern view of OD. Now there is acknowledgement of the relationship between participants in the decision making process, but also the importance of the relationship of the decision makers to the environment. As the mechanistic model of decision making in service of efficiency is left behind, OD finds itself needing to address as a serious question and concern the issue of *the personhood of the OD practitioner* (Eisen, 2010). The shift toward a more *relational* perspective on decision making will have profound implications for both theory and practice.

Figure 1 below depicts the contrasting perspectives on decision making between traditional OD shaped by a mechanistic view of the world and modern OD shaped by a more relational perspective.

Decision Making in Modern OD	Decision Making in Traditional OD
Decision making is oriented toward meaning-making and transformation that supports communities of practice.	Decision making is to be shared to the extent necessary and gatekeeping of information is considered appropriate.
Focus on deep change	Focus on quick fix
Focus on the group as valuable for generating good ideas.	Focus is on the individual as performer or actor and individual expertise
Focus on mindfulness and self-awareness	Focus on knowledge of facts and expertise
Mobility across boundaries may result in positive outcomes	Boundary spanning activity is considered to be problematic
Seek organization-environment symbiosis	Environment is a threat if it is not controlled
Diversity is valued and leads to rich array of perspectives	Diversity is a potential threat and may enhance instability
Experience of new cultures enriches consciousness and deepens awareness	Ideal is to be culture-free. Organizations and management are to be culture neutral

Figure 1. The shift in decision making from traditional OD to the modern OD perspective reflects the shift from the modern to the postmodern worldview

The Great Promise of Consensus Decision Making

"There is no formal leadership structure among the San bushmen community. Decisions are arrived at by consensus and issues are deliberated upon and discussed communally. Certain roles may require leadership from individuals with expertise such as hunting. No single group member holds positions of general influence over the rest of the community. This set up proved to be problematic to white colonialists when they wanted to enter into agreements..."

Rhizome: A Brief History of Consensus Decision Making

Consensus decision making may be as old as human decision making (Rhizome, 2011). It can be found in records of decision making processes of indigenous peoples around the world, including the San 'bushmen' of South Africa. Sometimes described as *simple consensus,* this approach contains the simple assumption that, if a decision is to be good for all involved, it needs to be agreed to by all involved. It is important to note that in both indigenous communities that practice simple consensus and in later practices of consensus--such as evidenced among the Religious Society of Friends (Quakers) (Sheeran, 1996) and other faith communities --there is a priority placed on *relationship* over outcome. It is important to distinguish here that *simple consensus* in this context is different from what we may understand as *unanimous agreement*. In the oldest and deepest sense of consensus, it means more than no one disagreeing with a decision brought forward by an individual within a group. Rather, it carries the sense that there is *collective wisdom* or understanding emerging from the group as a whole that transcends the individual knowledge or perspective of any single individual. The positivistic orientation of decision making literature where decision making is viewed as finding agreement among *individuals* in regard to a specific advanced *agenda* makes it challenging to even frame this notion.

> **The Value of Group Agreement in Sacred Texts**
>
> In sacred texts from the major religions of the world, agreement of the group is held as a great spiritual value.
>
> ٱلْجَمَاعَةُ رَحْمَةٌ.
>
> **With group lies Divine mercy.**

The wisdom of agreement within the group is an essential component of sacred texts from the major religions of the world. It calls forward the sense that the decision must be for the highest good or greatest purpose. It mitigates against the self-interest voice of a single individual or a number of individuals within a group. For groups interested in deepening understanding of decision making as a way of finding *shared higher purpose*, there is great value in starting with the sacred texts and spiritual teachings of the major religions of the world as well as with the body of what can be called *wisdom* literature.

Agreement-reaching as a Spiritual Value

"Another way to say what I mean is this: If two of you...are in balanced agreement with each other, exemplifying the harmony of the heavens (the communion of wave, sound, and name), then anything which you ask in that communal mind—tranquil, straightforward, without deception—will occur by the power that gave me birth, by the Breathing Life of All, the Mother-Father of the Cosmos."

A translation of Mathew 18:19 in Aramaic from the Peshitta (Assyrian and Syrian Orthodox Christian) version of the Gospels From *Desert Wisdom* (1995).

Agreement Reaching in the Society of Friends (Quakers)

"There is that near you which will guide you. O wait for it and be sure that ye keep to it."

Isaac Penington, An Early Quaker. From his 99th

But *consensus decision making* has come to mean something very different in both research and practice in the modern organizational context. It has been popularized as an enhancement for making decision making more *participatory* within the context of institutions that may promote it while at the same time solidifying social, political, and cultural barriers to any perspective that serves as an obstacle or alternative to the predominant voice.

Facilitators, with good intentions of increasing the participation of individuals in a group process or wanting to ensure that 'all voices are heard,' may turn to *formal consensus* as a tool. Often, consensus is promoted as an approach that can work as an adjunct to other decision making models. Proponents of formal consensus bring forward the intent to balance the long-held desire for *efficiency* in decision making with the promise of a process that is *fair, collaborative,* and to "involve every person who is affected by the decision in the decision making process" (Butler, 1987, p. 3). Consensus decision making is currently being promoted as a tool for use of any organization to promote a sense of participation "regardless of whether the final decision-making power rests with a single person or team, a vote of members or unanimity" (Hartnett, 2011). The approach promises *widespread agreement*. It considers consensus to be an approach rather than a methodology.

Formal consensus is a process where there is general discussion around an issue or concern followed by a *call for consensus*. This provides the opportunity for individuals to express *concerns* about the proposed decision. Concerns may then be addressed through further discussion or may be footnoted in the final outcome decision recorded by the group. In a formal consensus process failure to reach agreement may simply mean setting aside the agenda item and moving on to the next one (Butler, 1987).

While "shared decision-making is increasingly advocated as an ideal....decision-making process" (Charles, Whelan, Gafni, Willan, & Farrell, 2003, p. 689), even vocal proponents of the consensus model suggest that "the chances for reaching such a full agreement are rather low" and "complete agreement is not necessary in real life" (Herrera-Viedma, Herrera, & Chiclana, 2002, p. 394). How can an approach so promising at the same time be so disappointing?

5

The Pitfalls of Consensus Decision Making

"Important decisions may take too long to make, or the status quo may become virtually impossible to change. The resulting tension may undermine group functionality and harm relationships between group members."

Tim Hartnett from
Consensus-Oriented Decision Making

Research on consensus decision making over the past decades suggests that the outcome may often be group members simply agreeing to no longer disagree (Mahaffy, 2012). There may be no real unanimity and sense that the group and its purpose in meeting have been moved forward. It may leave participants in the process singularly unsatisfied.

"Then we are agreed nine to one that we will say our previous vote was unanimous!"

The question must be asked whether consensus models, as practiced in decision making processes today, really promote a *multi-lens* and *multi-vocal* (Anderson, 1997; McNamee & Gergen, 1999) dialogue. Are such processes sometimes used to assert a proposed shared position that is brought forward by one or more persons in positions of power? In that case, does consensus perhaps *enhance*, rather than minimize, hierarchical decision making? Hartnett's (2011) suggestion that the methods of consensus decision making can be used even in cases where "the final decision-making power rests with a single person" suggests this may be the case. His handbook on decision making suggests that a component of the step of finalizing a consensus decision is *showing empathy* for group members left unhappy by the outcome.

Consensus decision making takes to a new level a series of efforts to make decision making more inclusive and participatory. It furthers the notion that *top-down* decisions that do not engage those most affected by the outcome of the decision making process, may be both undesirable and ineffective. At the same time efforts, such as consensus models, to make decision making more participatory have been singularly disappointing to many. Has the trade-off of *efficiency* for *enhanced participation* led to better decisions? Many think not. On the one hand, there are those who suggest, along with the author, that power hierarchies are maintained and reinforced in complex ways that are not easily overcome simply by seeking greater group participation in decision making dialogues (M. Gergen, 2001). On the other hand, there are

> ## A Failed Exercise in Consensus Decision Making
>
> *Many years ago I was called in to facilitate an organization that was seeking to make a fundamental change in their organizational structure. Essentially, they were choosing to disassociate themselves from the national group with which they had been affiliated since their founding. I came in with good intentions of helping the group reach 'consensus' on this issue. After all, it was an important decision that the group hoped would be supported by all. It was supported by most. Paul was the single important hold-out. He had been involved since day one and could not support the change. The group went through a process of trying to listen to his concern through the normal consensus process. But he was adamant and unwilling to change his position. Setting aside the protocols for a consensus process, I asked for a time-out from decision making and asked Paul to share with me and the group his story of how the organization was first formed and his role. What evolved out of that story-sharing process was Paul's evident need to be acknowledged and thanked for his early formative work, before the group moved on to a new chapter. When he was able to receive that, Paul was able to let go of his objection to the change and move forward. His voice remained important and valued.*

those who believe that the effort at less hierarchical decision making is a failed experiment and return to a praise of the *efficiency* of hierarchical models (See Jaques (1990) *In Praise of Hierarchy*).

If the efforts to make decision making more participatory and less hierarchical have failed to change the fundamental role of decision making in organizational and societal relationships, the question must be asked *why is this so?* The author's research (Mahaffy, 2012) suggests this is the case because these efforts work from the same shared assumptions that have shaped decision making since industrial times that hold subject-object dualism at the center. As long as the design of decision making is understood in terms of two or more parties oppositionally engaged in a mental process of sharing information between them in an effort to find a *meeting ground* between them, the outcomes may be disappointing. Each person coming into a decision making process with this perspective, brings in their own world view, their own assumptions, their own beliefs. Mainstream decision making practice starts as a negotiating process over individual positions and beliefs to find some middle ground. In this paradigm, the essential components of the *situation* of decision making are a subject and an object, a speaker and a listener, and a mental or cognitive process whereby information is exchanged and positions negotiated. The language of dualism and division is evident. Decision making in this model starts out with an *agenda* and diverse parties coming to *work* that agenda with the intent of finding some agreement or meeting place. Often, the battle ground has been set even before the meeting has started.

Consensus decision making seeks to interject some *fairness* into this confrontation. It asks that the parties have equal time, listen to each other, and seek to find some compromise that everyone participating can agree on. Differences that cannot be resolved may be carried over to the next agenda. While consensus suggests that participating parties will get less hurt by this process it does expect that all parties will not leave fully satisfied. The literature of consensus acknowledges that the process may, in fact, need to be stopped before relationships are damaged. But what happens if we *start with the relationship(s) instead of starting with the agenda*? Let's explore that together and find out!

Finding our Way Forward: Beyond Consensus Decision Making

"That which is essential to all that we hold dear cannot be owned, penetrated, or articulated. In the consciousness of the relational we come to find a sacred potential."

Kenneth Gergen in
Relational Being: Beyond Self and Community

If we have *shaped* decision making in a certain way by our assumptions about what it is, might we agree to *reshape* that design for the purpose of "sustaining the …possibility of co-creating the good…toward a position of responsibility for relationships themselves (Gergen, 2009, p. 354)? To begin with *relationship* and *responsibility for relationship* in decision making, we must abandon starting with a *subject*, an *object*, and an *agenda*. In doing so, we are going against the fundamental tenants of the modern world-view as it relates to decision making. The modern world-view holds the subject-object relationship as primary. Decision making has, to this day, largely been unable to escape that frame. The postmodern worldview *de-centers* the subject opening the door for a more *fluid*, *life-giving*, and *generative* way of understanding decision making. We suggest that it may be time to evolve a decision making model that starts from a place other than subject-object relationships. Early works of social constructionism demonstrated clearly the "impasse of individual knowledge" (Gergen, 1994, p. 3) even when individual knowledge is placed into the setting of inter-personal decision making processes. This early work articulates well how a positivist view of knowledge leads to "hegemonic discourse" (p. 11)—a *single dominant conversation*. If participants within a decision making process come into a *dominant* discourse (conversation) there may be few opportunities for *alternative* discourses (conversations). Social psychology suggests that, in decision making processes, this sets the stage for the *fear of making mistakes* (Henriques, 1984) which can become a tool of control compelling participants not to deviate too greatly from the predominant discourse or view. How will we ever find our way forward to the transformational changes that our institutions and our world may need if we are to co-create a desired positive future?

Even the notion of *consensus* in decision making "rapidly reduces once again to the assumption of an inbuilt subjectivity of origin" (Urwin, 1984, p. 289). I suggest here that while consensus may provide some opening for alternative discourses to exist, it does not open the door wide for *alternative* discourses to replace *predominant* discourses. It may provide at best some opportunity for the two to co-exist in an uneasy embrace. I expect that every reader of this work on *Relational Presence* has experienced in their life, some time when there was a deep meeting of hearts and minds, where differences fell aside, and where a group decided to move forward together in a new and bold direction that fell outside of the predominant paradigm or popular way of thinking. If you have not, I hope you do! I suggest that this place is most easily found when we start with the *relationship* rather than the agenda in our decision making processes. Cannato (2006) presents a spiritually framed version of the notice of the *primacy of relationship:* "What nourishes any of us, more than bread itself, is a relationship in which we discover simultaneously who we are as we discover who the other is" (p. 138). In the world of ideas and the study of human engagement the notion of the *primacy of relationship* has been perhaps most clearly articulated by the relational-constructionist approach. We now turn there to consider how this approach shapes an understanding of decision making.

A Relational Constructionist Approach to Decision Making

"The major challenge of decision-making...is to mobilize collaborative processes in the service of effective action...it is through relational coordination that the organization comes to life."

Kenneth Gergen from
Relational Being: Beyond Self and Community

In the relational constructionist approach, *relationship* is primary (Gergen, 1994). A theory of knowing (epistemology) cannot meaningfully begin at a starting point other than *relationship*. A theory of being (ontology) cannot define existence apart from *relationship*. *Relationship* gives the context for a deepened and meaningful understanding of decision making. It provides a macro-lens for enlarging the view of the universe that is shrunk to less-than-life proportions in the empiricists' view of reality.

The implications of the relational constructionist approach for an understanding of decision making are profound. Instead of "decontextualized theory" (p. 135), the relational constructionist approach calls forward an "acute sensitivity to the perspectives of other peoples and times" (p. 137) and "generates a critical posture toward the taken-for-granted" (pp. 136-137). To the extent that this inquiry finds life in the relational constructionist approach, it will demonstrate "relational appreciation" (Mary Gergen, 1999, p. 107) for existing and historical decision making streams of practice, while at the same time seeking a "broad enrichment of theories, methods, and practices" (Ken Gergen, 1994, p. 138). The relational constructionist approach opens the door for a substantially different perspective on decision making because it starts with a radically different epistemology and ontology and a non-empiricist view of the organization, participants in organizational processes, contexts, and meaning making.

The relational constructionist approach brings forward the profound understanding that "discourse is not the possession of a single individual" but "meaningful language is the product of social interdependence" (Gergen, 1994, p. viii). First identified as *social constructionism* (Berger & Luckmann, 1966; Gergen, 1977; Gergen, 1985; Gergen, 1994) and later identified as *relational constructionism* (Hosking & Pluut, 2010; McNamee & Hosking, 2012), this approach breaks free from the "individualist view of knowledge exemplified by contemporary cognitive psychology" (Gergen, 1994, p. ix).

In the relational constructionist context, *meaning* is relationally constructed. It is an on-going and flowing process. "Relationships of interdependency" and "meaningful language is the product of social interdependence" (Gergen, 1994, p. viii). This understanding, that moves knowledge beyond the context of an individual subject, is at the core of the relational constructionist perspective. Social reality, organizational life, and decision making are products of "communal construction" (p. 1).

Organizations, in the relational constructionist context can be viewed as semi-bounded entities brought together by a "communally shared narrative" (Gergen, 2009, p. 316). Organizations are more or less bounded depending on the extent to which they define themselves as distinct or apart from their larger cultural, social, and historical context. Organizations are more or less fluid to the extent that they allow or disallow the free movement of people, ideas, and expressions of *multiple voices.*

The relational constructionist approach builds on the postmodern view of the importance of organizational culture to add that "rather than viewing cultures as fixed entities, a relational view holds that 'culturing' is a continuously unfolding process" (p. 322).

Language is of paramount importance in the relational constructionist perspective on decision making. Gergen (2009) notes, along with others, that organizations do not exist outside of language. If organizations can be understood as "collaborative and contending discourses" (p. 322) decision making is viewed as a process of inclusive dialogues "giving voice to multi-being" (p. 325). It becomes clear why the metaphors of *voice* and the rich stream of *dialogue* and *collaborative practices* become so central to the relational constructionist lens on decision making. Gergen notes that here is where relational constructionism joins hands with the learning organization movement—decision making is not a closed process but a conversation that is "forever open" (p. 331).

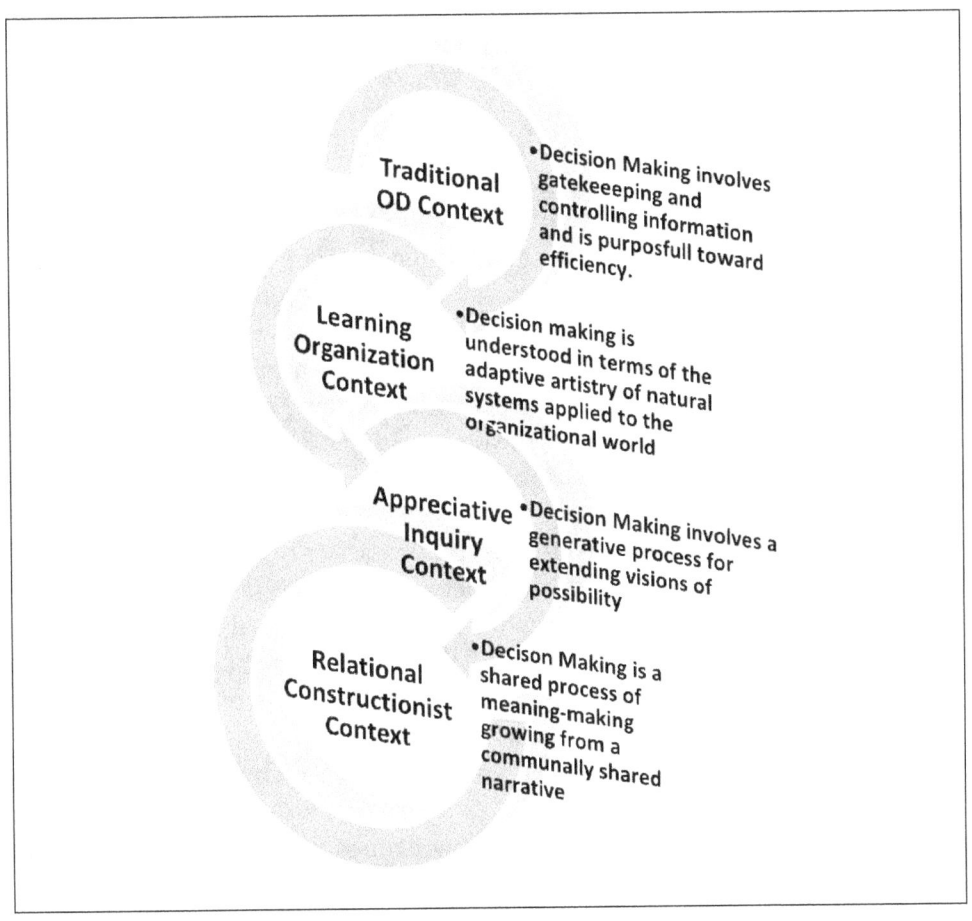

The relational constructionist approach describes "decision-making as relational coordination" (Gergen, 2009, p. 320). In this view, "the major challenge of decision-making…is to mobilize collaborative processes in the service of effective action. Gergen notes that "it is through relational coordination that the organization comes to life" (p. 312). Building on the notion that *relationship* is primary, we now ask if there is more involved in decision making than *relational coordination* among individuals. Can we talk about *relationships* with the *world(s)* in which our decision making happens? Can we talk about decision making not only in terms of discourses among human participants, but a conversation *with the situation itself?*

Moving Beyond Relational Coordination in Decision Making

"Within adversarial contexts...the idea of reflective practice leads to a vision of professionals as agents of society's reflective conversation with its situation."

Donald Schön
The Reflective Practitioner: How Professionals Think in Action

Is decision making more than relational coordination among human actors? The author's research suggest the importance of *absent participants, non-human actors/actants,* and the *situation itself* as components of decision making processes (Mahaffy, 2012). Schön (1983) articulates an intriguing notion of how human participants *design* space by their interaction with it. Schön understands "design as a reflective conversation with the situation" (p. 76). In terms of Schön's framework, the *design* of decision making can be understood as a process of the *interactive engagement* of the decision maker(s) with the *situation*. The designer (decision maker) "shapes the situation in accordance with his initial appreciation of it, the situation 'talks back,' and he responds to the situation's back-talk" (p. 79) creating a "reflective conversation with the situation" (p. 353). In this expanded view, the discourses of decision making are no longer restricted to the predominant and alternative discourses of human participants (speakers and listeners) but also inclusive of the group's *reflective conversation with the situation itself*. It is a perspective that radically moves decision making beyond a subject-object dualism, but also suggests that something larger is going on than relational coordination among human actors and participants.

It is congruent with Schön's approach to describe the situation of decision making as constructed by the reflective interaction and conversation between the *decision makers* and the *situation itself*. "Through his transaction with the situation, (the decision maker) shapes it and makes himself a part of it. Hence, the sense he makes of the situation must include his own contribution to it. Yet he recognizes that the situation, having a life of its own distinct from his intentions, may foil his projects and reveal new meanings" (p. 163). The interaction with the situation will have less to do with a "body of techniques" and more to do with "an art, a matter of skill and wisdom" (p. 237).

This perspective dramatically changes the way we view decision making. The role of the expert, the facilitator, and the leader become far less important if decision making is less about a *body of techniques* and more *a matter of art, of skill, and of wisdom*. The *emergence of new meanings and* the sense we make of the situation may take on greater importance than the specific decisions that are made by a community or group. We remember the 'bushmen' of South Africa who would not move forward in their 'negotiations' with colonialists, until there was shared understanding and agreement among all in their community as to the situation they were facing with their world being turned upside down by outsiders.

In a Western context, decision making is often distanced from *lived experience*. It may be hard to imagine decision makers in a corporate boardroom having a reflective conversation with the situation! So to illustrate what this might look like and how it might affect the outcome of

The Hyena Man of Harar: A Reflective Conversation with the Situation

Villagers in Ethiopia and Eritrea sometimes find the hyenas encroaching on their village from the surrounding hills, endangering chickens, livestock, and perhaps even young children. While the impulse is sometimes to want to poison the hyenas or fight back against them, a centuries old tradition has come forward from the village of Harar. There, a decision was made long ago, to respond a different way and to consider that the hyenas were neighbors encroaching on the village because of their hunger. From sacred teachings in the village, the tradition was started to have the designated *Hyena Man of Harar* visit with the hungry hyenas in the hills outside the village. He would be engaged in a conversation with them, acknowledging their need and responding by feeding them meat provided by the villagers. The hyenas would sometimes take raw meat from the mouth of the Hyena man. Villagers deeply believe that this *reflective conversation with the situation* leads to peace between the hyenas and the villagers.

decision making process, we turn to an illustration from African villages in Ethiopia and the story of the Hyena Man of Harar. It presents a lens on what a reflective conversation with the situation, involving both human and non-human participants might look like.

What does it mean to have a *reflective conversation with the situation* in decision making today? I find that it means a *shared collective awareness* or *appreciation* of our collective situation. This leads us to *pause* before an intellectual or verbal response. I put forward that it means opening the door to the *deep learning* that may come through reflectively taking inventory of our situation and its sometimes stunning complexity. This may mean *reflecting* on the conversations and discourses that have preceded this one-- the historical, social, cultural, and political context in which we find ourselves. It may lead us to a *heightened awareness* of complexities that mitigates against hasty and rash responses or action. It may require self-reflective relation, not only with the participants in the room in the decision making process, but also holding in awareness those who are not present, the non-human actors, the communities, the generations, the future that may be impacted by the decisions we make. It may involve a conversation with *future generations* -- taking the seventh generation test of sustainability, as did the Iroquois clans, to consider the impact of their decisions seven generations down the road. It may mean asking not only how our decisions affect those in the room, but also how they affect our environment. The *conversation with the situation* may bring forward profound considerations of *sustainability* and *stewardship* and also of ethical considerations in decision making. The reflective conversation says, *it is not only about us,* but gives consideration to all our relations.

Relational constructionism suggests that we *construct* our world from social and relational materials. Might it be that equally important is sometimes to engage in *friendly disentangling* (Nielson, 1998) of relationships gone wrong to being reconstructing more sustainable ones?

Accepting Disagreement and Differences

"No point of view has the whole story. Reality is deeper than any story, so it's valuable to have multiple perspectives available to help us see more deeply into any situation. My suggestion is that we fully embrace the reality that people disagree."

Todd Duncan: Glimpses of Wonder

Consensus decision making, as it is practiced today, is in large part driven by a compelling interest in finding *agreement*. Facilitators, OD consultants, church leaders, and political leaders are joined by professionals from the practices of mediation and conflict resolution in searching for effective strategies to get to *agreement*. Todd Duncan suggests that we should be asking "how can we create a structure within which differing views can peacefully coexist and learn from each other for the betterment of all" (Duncan, 2012).

> **Respecting Differences as Relational Beings**
>
> *"Teaching tolerance was anathema to Gandhi. People, he felt, should not tolerate each other and their differences, but learn to respect, understand, accept and appreciate each other. Only through a strong and respectful relationship can we have peace and harmony within ourselves and in our society."*
>
> Arun Gandhi,
> Gandhi's Grandchild

Relational constructionism offers a context for allowing such peaceful coexistence of oppositional views with its invitation into a "multivoiced" (McNamee & Gergen, 1999, p. 12) perspective on decision making. Harlene Anderson (1997) notes that disagreements often rise to the level of what she calls *"dueling realities"* (p. 74). She suggests allowing the space for "the coexistence of multiple realities" (p. 75) as a way to avoid impasse. I find particularly life-giving, Harlene Anderson's perspective that, while Western culture is particularly resistant to the idea of just accepting disagreement, the process of discovering and accepting differences can be a way of giving ourselves permission to take on some new maps and create the possibility for transformational change (conversation with Harlene Anderson cited in Mahaffy, 2012). From this perspective, *breakthroughs* in decision making processes are not so much when participants reach agreements, but rather when participants together find ways of *ascribing new shared meanings to their situations and circumstances*.

Accepting Differences

I was surprised to run in to Jessica and Jeff at the county fair. They were delighting in sharing cotton candy with their five year old son Caleb. Only nine months before, they had come into my office for divorce mediation. As a mediator approved by the Idaho Supreme Court for family mediation, I had helped them devise the parenting plan they needed in order to get their divorce filed in the Idaho courts. There had been a contentious battle over property. Most of the equity in their home had gone toward paying their respective lawyers to argue in court over division of their dwindling community property. In our three mediation sessions, I had asked Jessica and Jeff to imagine that the round table we sat around was a campfire in the desert. I asked them to imagine by this campfire that they were parting ways after a long journey together across the desert on their camels. As they went their separate ways as they had chosen to do, 'what did they want to take forward that was most precious from their shared journey as a couple?' They both agreed it was their together-time with their son Caleb. It was evident when I met them at the county fair that this now-divorced couple had found a place to honor their differences while still finding ways to continue sharing that which had been most precious to them. Today, that meant eating cotton candy together at the county fair.

Perhaps decision making processes might be viewed less as engaging in a conversation to find agreement on some *truth* and more as a process of *deepening* together. Fundamentalism and religious dogma present a *truth* to which everyone must subscribe and the consequences of failing to do so may be religious wars or what are sometimes characterized as *holy wars*. But it is in the spirit of the sacred texts of the world religions, not to seek to obliterate differences, but to not have those differences become an obstacle to shared higher purpose. The great evening prayer Khatum asks not that differences be obliterated, but asks "raise us above the distinctions and differences that divide." It calls forward a meeting place above differences.

For many of us who are facilitators of decision making processes, there is a *bright and shiny ornament* that we seek as the outcome of that process. The prize is an *agreement*. After all, it's pleasant to agree! After having worked with more than five hundred nonprofit organizations, I have found that their *mission statements* can at times, be a great stumbling block. The *mission statement* of a nonprofit is its *bright and shiny ornament*. It is the reason the nonprofit exists, it is the shared beliefs that bind the members or participants together. It may be a creedal question, when the nonprofit hires a new employee and asks if they *are able to subscribe to the mission statement*. The trouble is that the times and contexts that drew forward the mission statement change. A mission statement may become a fixed belief from the past that becomes a hindrance to an organization finding its way forward and fulfilling those purposes and actions it cares most about.

Accepting of *differences* is an aspect of an approach to decision making that is *generative*. Generative processes recognize that both individuals and organizations, when they open to *self-awareness,* are always changing. Transformation is about our allowing both ourselves and our institutions to be different today than they were yesterday. *Generative mechanisms* are those that enhance "flourishing with organizations" (Spreitzer & Cameron, 2012, p. 1037). The *generative dynamics* that keep decision making always opening new meanings, new understandings, and deeper reflection and action, is an area that has been "largely uninvestigated" in organizational decision making (Spreitzer & Cameron, 2012, p. 4).

It is perhaps the greatest singular act of caring and intimacy as *relational beings* (Gergen, 2009) when we give to ourselves, to others, and to our organizations, the *permission to change*. In an intimate relationship, it is a loving act. Just before I left for Ghent, Belgium this past spring to participate in and present at the 5th Global Appreciative Inquiry Summit, my partner reflected to our twin daughters—*take a good look at your father. He will be a different person when he comes back from Belgium!* This loving stance gave permission for me to change and be changed, and for our relationships to change. Accepting that we may be different tomorrow, from who we are today, is the first step in transformational change. It is also the place where we discover together the *richness of relationship*.

Discovering the Richness of Relationship in Decision Making

"When the subject-object duality that is basic to our habitual awareness begins to dissolve, we shift from looking 'out at the world' from the viewpoint of a detached observer to looking from 'inside'...Martin Buber evocatively described this as a movement from an 'I-it' to an 'I-thou' relationship. In the 'I-thou' relationship what appears in our awareness is whole and exists in an intimate relationship with us."

From Presence: Human Purpose and the Field of the Future
by Senge, Scharmer, Jaworski, and Flowers

Moving beyond a dualistic framework in decision making opens the door for discovering the *richness of relationship*. That is because when we discover that decision making is *relationally constructed* there is the opportunity to choose the quality of the relationships that we have. When we truly take the opportunity to be *present* to each other in decision making processes, there is the opportunity for *intimacy*. The notion of *intimacy* is becoming an acceptable topic in the arena of decision making. Kark (2012) lays out many of the issues in regard to this under-explored area. To accept the possibility that organizational relationships might be such that individuals "have real sensitivity to what matters to others" (p. 424), is to accept that there may be a way to discover *intimacy* in decision making. How will this affect the way in which we make decisions?

If intimacy can be described as coming from the place of the heart, instead of from the head, decision making will, in the opinion of Zukav (1996) come from the place of the *heart* and not from the *intellect*. "The mind will no longer be the focus, the 'leader' in the old sense. Decision making will be intuitive. The logic and understanding utilized will be the higher order of

Moving From 'Active Listening' to 'Relational Listening'

'Active listening' increases mutual understanding. The speaker and listener demonstrate understanding by feeding back what they have heard. It is a great exercise and a valuable skill for effective communication. But 'relational listening' goes beyond that. It is about 'listening together' or 'discerning' to deepen relationship. It allows new shared meanings to emerge from intersubjective knowledge where neither the subject, the object, nor the social is at center stage.

> **From Burden to Blessing: How the Shift From Focus on Agenda to Focus on Relationship Transformed a Nonprofit Mission**
>
> *Six years ago I led an Appreciative Inquiry (AI) process for a nonprofit serving homeless families. This coalition of thirty churches in the community was at a crisis point. Board membership, community participation, and financial resources were all dwindling. During a day-long visioning process stakeholders began to speak of the deepest motivations that brought them to give so much to this ministry. From these stories there emerged a subtle, yet profound shift in the way that the organization looked at its mission. The focus shifted in an almost imperceptible way. Instead of seeing itself as an organization that 'exists to minister to the homeless' there emerged a sense of the organization as one that exists to "share the blessing we have experienced in working with homeless families to regain their independence.' The relationships with homeless families and how new meanings and understandings had emerged from these relationships became the focus. The conversation shifted from the burden and obligation to care for homeless families to the blessing of the richness of the relationship. The organization was able to move forward with new-found energy and appreciation.*

logic and understanding of the heart" (p. 324). There has been little exploration of decision making from the place of heart-intimacy. It touches on the rich literature of *heart-knowledge* (Huebner, 1999). While human interactions from the place of the heart have been studied from the perspective of teaching (Rinderknecht, 2004) there would be richness in exploring more deeply the motif of decision making from the place of the heart and heart-intimacy.

When we uncover the richness of relationship the focus may shift from prioritizing the *agenda* to prioritizing the *relationship*. This move beyond *intersubjectivity* opens the door for *listening together* and deciding together. The process of *listening together* can be illustrated in the practice of *discernment,* as exercised by the Quakers as well as by other streams of practice, where religious beliefs are deeply connected to *action* in the world to serve others.

The concept of *discernment* is distinctly different from the practice of *consensus* as that is understood by most practitioners today. Consensus involves an iterative process of actively listening to each other's concerns until some point of agreement emerges. Ideas are exchanged in an environment that encourages all present to speak and share any objections they may have to a proposed decision. *Discernment* is subtly, but distinctly different. Instead of *listening to each other* it involves *listening together.* It requires stepping outside of a subject-object, speaker-listener dualism. The notion of *discernment* introduces to the situation of decision making complexities of relationship with both participants and with their internal and external, shared and unshared universes of discourse, and complexities of relationship with the situation itself. The discernment process shapes the spatiality of decision making in the Quaker meetinghouse where the focus is not on any individual or even on the group. The focus is on listening for *leading* and for *guidance* as that is understood in either a religious or a non-religious sense. *Discernment* stands outside the constructs of knowledge as a rational or mental process.

The process of listening *together* or *relational listening* leads to developing together an *image of the future.* *The Image of the Future by* Fred Polak (1973) helped to shape the constructs of AI. Polak describes the *image of the positive* as emerging from "beholding with the inward eye…a sensitivity to and communication with the unseen" (p. 271). It emerges from the place of *presence.*

Discovering Relational Presence in Decision Making

"The poetry from the Native American tradition references 'woniya wakan.' It is the 'holy air' in the Lakota language—their translation of Holy Spirit. It is that which renews all by its breath. It is spirit, life, breath, renewal. It is the felt-space between us, the presence in our midst. It is something sacred, holy, or something incomprehensible that is there when decisions are made together reflecting a shared higher purpose. It is relational breath, because it is the air that is shared and breathed by all living creatures. It is the holy air that connects us all and it is the reminder that any decisions made must be made for the good of all our relation."

From Samuel Mahaffy
Relational Presence in Decision Making

Finding our Capacity for Communion in the Place of Presence

"What nourishes any of us, more than bread itself, is a relationship in which we discover simultaneously who we are as we discover who the other is. Communion that honors the other, that reverences the Holy One in the other and in the self—this is what we embrace. Connectedness is primary. Communion is essential."

Judy Cannato
Radical Amazement

In the author's research on breakthrough decision making, the notion of *presence* emerges as a significant constituent theme (Mahaffy, 2012). It appears in both sacred and secular literature alike. It is a notion that is essential if we are to move beyond dualisms and toward a more integral view of decision making. The term first gains prominence in the literature of OD and decision making with the publication of *Presence: Human Purpose and the Field of the Future* (Senge, Scharmer, Jaworksi, Flowers, 2004). In their work, *presencing* involves developing "a capacity to let go and surrender our perceived need to control" (p. 96). It involves being "an instrument of life itself" and a "future seeking to emerge" (p. 228). This language mirrors the early social constructionist metaphor of the *invitation to a dance* as a descriptor of human interaction in decision making and group contexts (Anderson, 1997; Gergen, 1994).

The notion of *presence* requires us to abandon any remnants of subject-object duality. Beyond the speaker and the listener, the subject and the object, is the felt-presence of the *in-between-ness* that is neither subject nor object and cannot be defined in terms of intersubjectivity. It is the *woniya wakan* or *holy air* described in the

Relational Presence in Decision Making: Redesigning the Spatiality of Decision Making

The architecture, the structure of assembly, the intent of convening are currently born of the leadership mind. This steals accountability from us all. It reinforces isolation and passivity. We need to redesign concrete and convention to be as a communal undertaking."

Peter Block in
From Leadership to Citizenship

"We know how to create spaces that invite the <u>intellect</u> to show up...we know how to create spaces that invite the <u>emotions</u> into play...we know how to create spaces that invite the <u>will</u> to emerge...we certainly know how to create spaces that invite the <u>ego</u> to put in an appearance, polishing its image, protecting its turf and demanding its rights. But we know very little about creating spaces that invite the <u>soul</u> to make itself known."

Parker Palmer
A Hidden Wholeness: The Journey Toward an Undivided Life

Lakota language as that which is not seen, but felt-- the space between us that we feel as a *presence*.

For those of us who live and breathe mainstream Western ontologies and epistemologies, the notion of *in-between-ness* that is neither subject nor object may be hard to grasp. But there is an intriguing and little-recognized stream that brings forward a rich perspective in this regard. In the philosophical ethics of Watsuji Tetsuro, recognized as one of the leading thinkers on ethics in Japan (Watsuji, 1992), the term *aidagara* is used to understand the notion of *betweeness*.

Arisaka (2001) notes that for Watsuji the 'field' is that place of coexistence between a person and society and that humans cannot ontologically be defined apart from this *space between*. In terms of both *being* and *knowing*—in terms of *ontology* and of *epistemology*—this is a place that is neither *self* nor *other*, but the place where the two *co-emerge*.

This sense of a place that is neither *self* nor *other* in terms of being and knowing is not restricted to eastern philosophy. For Martin Buber (1937) also, there is ontological reality to the space that lies between *I* and *thou*. While Western philosophy and science have paid little attention to that which is between subjectivity and objectivity, it is an area in which phenomenology has made some rich probing investigations (Zahavi, 2001). De Quincey (2000) describes this as *second person inquiry* which will lead to the *science of the heart*.

This understanding of knowledge leads us back to the primacy of *relationship* and a view of decision making that opens exciting new possibilities. The knowledge that evolves from the decision making knowledge, in this context, has little to do with knowledge for *control* and much to do with knowledge in service of *relationship*. De Quincey (2000) articulates the perspective this way: "We could say that standard third-person inquiry leads to a science of external bodies, first-person inquiry to an interior science of the mind, while second-person inquiry leads to a communal science of the heart" (p. 53). Particularly significant to an understanding of decision making from outside of a subject-object frame, he adds: Whereas the ultimate ideal of objective knowledge is control, and the ultimate ideal of subjective knowledge is peace, the ultimate ideal of inter-subjective knowledge is relationship" (p. 53).

If we are first *relational* beings (Gergen, 2009) this present work invites us to consider what it means to be *relational decision makers* where we experience *presence* because we show up as full human beings (not reduced to our rational selves) and where we practice *relational listening* that beyond active listening involves *listening together* and together having a *reflective conversation with the situation*. The findings from our research suggest that there are a number of essential components to this approach that we identify as *relational presence* in decision making. These components might be the building blocks of decision making re-designed—not toward the primacy of *efficiency* nor toward the primacy of *maximizing participation,* but toward the honoring of the *primacy of relationship*. We depict these components of *relational presence* as they relate to decision making in Figure 2 below:

Figure 2. Relational Presence

Relational Presence can be described as having no agenda, because it is the agenda. The agenda is to *show up*, to be present, to be honoring of the relationships. Participants in decision making from the place of *relational presence* are a *gathered community,* so named for their *attentiveness* to each other, to the situation itself, and to relationships broadly understood to be inclusive of both those physically present in the room and those absent. *The stranger* is welcomed to decision making in relational presence. In welcoming the stranger, we may well be unknowingly welcoming *wisdom.* In fact, in *relational presence* there is the sense that we are *all strangers* to each other, because we let go of our presumptions that we know each other. In the discourses of *relational presence* there is as much value given to silence as there is to speaking. In fact, silence may be more valuable than speaking. It may be that place of *quiet presence* where we re-find our center, our hidden wholeness. As far as knowledge, in relational presence *unknowing* is valued as much as *knowing. Unknowing* is invited. *Uncertainty* is certainly

> **Designing Decision Making for Respecting Relationships**
>
> *"Unfortunately, community in our culture too often means a group of people who go crashing through the woods together, scaring the soul away. In spaces ranging from congregations to classrooms, we preach and teach, assert and argue, claim and proclaim, admonish and advise, and generally behave in ways that drive everything original and wild into hiding. Under these conditions, the intellect, emotions, will, and ego may emerge, but not the soul; we scare off all the soulful things like respectful relationships...A circle of trust is a group of people who know how to sit quietly 'in the woods' with each other and wait for the shy soul to show up. The relationships in such a group are not pushy but patient; they are not confrontational but compassionate; they are filled not with expectations and demands but with abiding faith in the reality of the inner teacher and in each person's capacity to learn from it."*
>
> Parker Palmer in
> A Hidden Wholeness

present. So is the *certainty* of the voice of our soul, allowed to finally show up and speak with *courage*. Permission is given to make mistakes. The *atmosphere* of relational presence is thinner than thin air. It is the *ethers*, the *holy air, wonija wakan*. It is life itself, spirit, breath, renewal. It is the presence we feel between us. It is easy to breathe, because it is *quietly inviting*. It is *the presence in our midst*. Relationships are central. But they cannot be held still long enough to be defined as *subject* and *object* because they are always moving. This is the *mimetic movement*, where decision making is not so much positions, statements, and responses, but the *call* and the *echo of the call* of our souls and of our relationships with all our relations.

Decision making in *relational presence* may have to do less with finding *truth* or coming to the *right* decision and more with a process of going ever deeper with each other in relationship to allow new meanings, new understandings, and new perspectives to *emerge* from a creative, sorting, and energizing process. Decision making processes in our organizational contexts often become about digging through stacks of agendas, bringing forward reams of information and sorting through differing opinions and perspectives to find something that will nourish our spirits and our organizations. To view another perspective on decision making, I turn for a metaphor to the practice of *winnowing*. As ancient as the cultures that first grew grain together to feed their families, *winnowing* is a communal activity of casting grain up into the wind, allowing the breeze to blow the chaff away and the grain to settle down. The practice of separating grain from chaff in Western cultures has come to be a metaphor for separating *truth* from *falsehood*, *good* from *bad*, and *worthwhile* from *worthless*. But the chaff is not a worthless part of the grain. It is the protective coat that surrounds and guards the kernel allowing it to reach full maturity. It is cast to wind in a communal relational process that celebrates the harvest in indigenous cultures.

I remember the process of *winnowing* in the village in which I grew up in Eritrea. It was a time of communal gathering, of working together. It was a process that brought the wind and the elements into play as an essential component of the food-gathering life of the village.

Winnowing in Senafe, Eritrea.

Whereas our Western interpretations of winnowing have come to be about separating good and evil, *relational presence* suggests that winnowing might be a better metaphor for an *ever-deepening* process that a community engages in together, seeking the *kernel* of what is most nourishing, most sustaining, and most life giving for the community as a whole.

Applying Relational Presence in Every Day Decision Making

"You have to show up first, you have to occupy some place together, before you can change anything"

Michael Collier, Lay Pastor
Organizer, *Occupy Tacoma Movement*

The foundational notion of dualism in the predominant view of decision making implies *separation*. It is this separation that leads to the battle and war metaphors that have dominated the discourse (conversations) about breakthrough decision making. Unfortunately, these metaphors have also dominated the discourse about peacemaking or *agreement finding*.

The paradigm brought forward here, suggests that we start from the place of wholeness, rather than from the place of brokenness. Albert Einstein suggested that the notion of separation is perhaps a delusion: "A person experiences life as something separated from the rest—a kind of optical delusion of consciousness. Our task must be to free ourselves from this self-imposed prison, and through compassion, to find the reality of Oneness."

We bring forward the notion of *relational presence* as a core understanding of how we come to breakthrough decision making that represents a shared higher purpose. We suggest that this notion allows us to "move beyond cause and effect in understanding relationships" (Gergen, 2009, p. xvi) in the situation of decision making. This may lead to "restoring the relational

> **12 ASPECTS OF PRACTICING RELATIONAL PRESENCE IN EVERYDAY DECISION MAKING**
>
> 1. Primacy of Relationships
> 2. Quietly Inviting
> 3. Letting Go of Assumptions
> 4. Coming Together as a Gathered Community
> 5. Welcoming the Stranger
> 6. Valuing Silence
> 7. Relational Listening
> 8. Peripheral Vision
> 9. Mimetic Movement
> 10. Unknowing
> 11. Intimacy
> 12. Relational Presence is the Agenda

flow" (p. 192) that leads to "transformative dialogue" bringing forward "potentials for multi-being" (p. 193).

If we have designed decision making in a way that more often than not does not lead to *wholeness*, perhaps it is time to re-design it. This inquiry suggests that it may be urgent to do so as a "communal undertaking" (Block, 1998, p. 91). Growing out of my research (Mahaffy, 2012) I suggest that there are twelve aspects that shape *relational presence* as a pathway to decision making:

1. **Primacy of Relationships.** Very simply, *relationships* come first. They are the reason for decision making. Care for relationships determines how and why decisions are made. Relationships come before knowledge, before information, and these are understood as being relationally constructed.

2. **Quietly Inviting.** Research on the experience of teaching from an open and engaged heart (Rinderknecht, 2004) suggests that a teacher coming from the place of heart has a "way of being quietly, authentically present and inviting" (p. 130). Our findings are similar for decision making. *Relational presence* calls forward a receptivity that *welcomes the other*, invites the engagement, and *honors the relationship* in a way that is quiet and still and reflective of a *centered presence*.

> **Relational Listening**
>
> *We are haunted by our yearning to be addressed, by our need to listen. We are created for listening. It is our proper business. We are made for communion, but the communion for which we are formed is not that of mindless camaraderie. We yearn to come to terms by listening.*
>
> Walter Brueggemann
> Finally Comes the Poet: Daring Speech for Proclamation

3. **Letting Go of Assumptions.** By putting forward the priority of *in-between-ness* over the "I" and the "you"—the subject and the object—*relational presence* calls forward a *letting go of assumptions*. If we view decision making as a relational activity of allowing new meanings to emerge, there will not be room for holding forward assumptions about either the *other* or the *situation*.

4. **Coming Together as a Gathered Community.** A *gathered* meeting is one in which participants come together with the intent on being present to each other. They are *attentive*. There has been valuable work done on the importance of being *self-aware* and *other-aware* in decision making processes (Stavros & Torres, 2008). We suggest here the importance of being *community-aware*. What are the values that bring us together as a community?

5. **Welcoming the Stranger.** When we invite in *the stranger* in a decision making process, we are inviting in the possibility of new wisdom and understanding. Harlene Anderson

> **Silence on Fire**
>
> *"I will try...*
> *to be my own silence;*
> *And this is difficult. The whole*
> *world is secretly on fire...*
>
> *...How can one be still or*
> *Listen to all things burning?*
> *How can he dare*
> *To sit with them when*
> *All their silence*
> *Is on fire?*
>
> *Thomas Merton*
> *The Strange Islands: Poems*

references this as the notion of the *host/guest* (Anderson, 1997; Mahaffy, 2012). The literature of decision making gives little attention to the notion of *the stranger*. It is our expectation that decision making happens in institutional and organizational settings where participants are familiar to each other. Georg Simmel (1972) brought forward some of the first insightful discussions of the concept of *the stranger* as a participant in social interactions. *Relational presence* has particular attentiveness to the *gift of the stranger* (Smith and Carvill, 2000) in the decision making context.

6. **Valuing Silence.** *Silence* can have multiple and complex meanings. It may reflect *withdrawal* of participants in decision making processes. It may indicate that voices are being intentionally silenced. Or it may be silent protest of a predominant view. In this work, the valuing of silence means the valuing of the notion of *quiet presence*. This may be the place of *action* as much as of *inaction*.

7. **Relational Listening.** More than *active listening* to verify understanding, *relational listening* involves *listening together* for the emergence of new meanings.

8. **Peripheral Vision.** The notion of *peripheral vision* comes up in terms of the metaphor of the d*ance floor* as an image of relational engagement (Anderson, 1997; Gergen, 1994; McNamee & Gergen, 1999). It is deepened as a construct in later inquiries (Mahaffy, 2012). While dancing with one partner you may see other potential partners to dance with and movement all around you with peripheral vision. As explained to the author by a Moslem sheikh, the communal prayers in this faith involve praying standing in a row so that prayers are not focused on each other but are aware in their *peripheral vision* that there are others praying in the continuum of space around him or her. It is the sense that the supplicant is not praying *alone*. In *relational presence* we do not focus on the *other*, any more than we focus on the *self*, but we turn toward purpose, toward relationship, toward the situation, holding in awareness, through our *peripheral vision* that we are never alone.

9. **Mimetic Movement.** The notion of *mimetic movement* also grows from the metaphor of the *dance floor* as the place of relational engagement. It calls us to step completely outside of the predominant construct of decision making as *cause* and *effect*. subject and object. The notion of *mimetic movement* carries the sense of *relationship* as integral to the decision making process.

It holds some notion of the "looking glass self" (Gergen, 2009, p. xvii) but it goes beyond that. The notion is implied in Urwin's (1984) understanding in regard to how a child learns language. She suggests an alternative view to the notion that the child learns language through "mapping language onto cognition or action" (p. 283). Rather than viewing language learning as children "taking up subjective positions, which were previously occupied by significant adults" (p. 283) Urwin suggests the notion of *co-occurrence*. The interactions contained within the engagement of a very young child with a parent—instead of being viewed as a child *imitating* (stimulus-response) with social and linguistic skills thereby being transferred from parent to child—might be viewed as "playful interactions" of "relational positioning" (p. 292-293). In short, Urwin describes this infant-adult engagement in terms of what we call here a sort of *mimetic movement*. I bring forward the notions of *co-occurrence, playful interactions of relational positioning,* and *mimetic movement* are rich descriptors for *relational presence* in decision making.

10. **Unknowing.** The place of *unknowing* is valued as much or more than the *knowing* of experts and expertise. The notion of *unknowing* suggests the aspect of decision making as a *journey* that may involve uncertainty and faith. *The Cloud of Unknowing* (1981) is a little known book that is on the surface about contemplative prayer, but also is about a way of being in the world together. In his introduction to this little book, Tim Farrington, a Catholic who left his religious stream to practice Zen Buddhism, describes this as the "unmistakable voice of someone who has experienced 'God' beyond all baggage and disputes" (p. viii). Appreciative Inquiry has been described as a *journey* to discover a desired future which has a *positive image* that can lead to *action* at its core (Cooperrider, 2003). This is a descriptor that resonates with the notion of decision making as a *journey of discovery together into the unknown.* Polak (1973) suggests that this moves us from *diagnosis* to *prognosis*. The image of the future "not only indicates alternative choices and possibilities, but actively promotes certain choices and in effect puts them to work in determining the future" (p. 300).

11. **Intimacy.** Decision making comes from the place of the *heart* rather than the *head*. We get out of our heads in the sense that the mind is no longer the leader. While we may bring into decision making great intellectual capacity, the highest order of logic and understanding will come from the heart. From this place, decision making can be more intuitive and more tuned to relationship. It will be an experience of intimacy, maybe even when we least expect it!

12. **Relational Presence is the Agenda.** Finally, we note that decision making in *relational presence* does not *have* or *hold* an agenda, because relational presence *is* the agenda. It does not mean that an agenda does not emerge as an aspect of emerging meanings. Not only may agendas for discussion emerge, but also agendas for *action*. This notion of action *emerging* in and through and as an integral component of a *relational* process has sometimes been identified as *affirmation mysticism* (Caffrey, 1967). This is mysticism in the sense of a shared inner journey. But this is an inner life that reaches outward in service instead of inward in terms of isolation and withdrawal from the world (Jones, 1963). It is grounded and nurtured in action involving the "spiritualizing life here and now" (Caffrey, 1967, pp. 194-195). It has been referred to as the

"divine YES" (p. 207)—that place where decision making reaches completion and fulfillment only in service to others and to the community.

This inquiry proposes abandoning the word *sacred* to describe that place where organizations and groups make breakthrough decisions reflecting a shared higher purpose. The word is too loaded with constructs from dualistic world-views that extend back to the Middle Ages and beyond. We offer instead the notion of *relational presence*. It is the place where we move beyond the *subject* and *object,* beyond *de-centering the subject,* to that place where we have a shared lived experience of *unitive being* (pike, 1982). It is a place where "we discover simultaneously who we are as we discover who the other is" (Cannato, 2006, p. 138). Here we move *beyond consensus decision making* to find in our relationships the same *wonder* as we find in black holes, supernovas and other wonders. In short, we find a way of decision making that involves what Cannato (2006) calls *radical amazement*.

References

Anderson, H. (1997). *Conversation, language, and possibilities: A postmodern approach to therapy.* New York: Basic Books.

Arisaka, Y. (2001). The ontological co-emergence of 'self and other' in Japanese philosophy. *Journal of Consciousness Studies,* 8 (5-7), 197-208.

Axelrod, E., Cady, S.H., & Holman, P. (2010). Whole system change: What it is and why it matters. In W.J Rothwell, J.M. Stavros, R.L. Sullivan, & A. Sullivan, (Eds.). *Practicing organization development: A guide for leading change.* (pp. 363-376). San Francisco: John Wiley and Sons, Inc.

Bartunek, J.M., & Woodman, R.W. (2012). The spirits of organization development, or why OD lives despite its pronounced death. In K.S. Cameron, & G.M. Spreitzer, (Eds.), The *Oxford handbook of positive organizational scholarship.* (pp. 727-736). New York: Oxford University Press.

Berger, P.L., & Luckmann, T. (1966). *The social construction of reality: A treatise in the sociology of knowledge.* New York: Doubleday.

Block, P. (1998). From leadership to citizenship. In L.C. Spears, (Ed.), Insights *on leadership: Service, stewardship, spirit, and servant-leadership.* (pp. 87–95). New York: John Wiley & Sons, Inc.

Bolman, L.G., & Deal, T.E. (2003). *Reframing organizations: Artistry, choice, and leadership.* San Francisco: Jossey-Bass.

Butler, C.T. (1987). *On conflict and consensus: A handbook on formal consensus decisionmaking.* Portland, ME: Food Not Bombs Publishing.

Caffrey, A.J. (1967). The *affirmation mysticism of Rufus Matthew Jones.* (Doctoral dissertation). Retrieved from University Microfilms, Inc., Ann Arbor, MI. (67-15,433).

Cannato, J. (2006). *Radical amazement: Contemplative lessons from black holes, supernovas, and other wonders of the universe.* Notre Dame, IN.: Sorin Books

Charles, C.A., Whelan, T., Gafni, A., Willan, A. & Farrell, S. (2003). Shared treatment decision making: What does it mean to physicians? *Journal of Clinical Oncology, Vol. 21, No. 5,* pp. 932-936.

Cloud of Unknowing. (1981). San Francisco: Harper.

Cooperrider, D.L. (2012). *Toward an 'economy' of connecting strength: Scaling up the generative power of AI.* Keynote presentation at the 2012 World Appreciative Inquiry Conference, Ghent, Belgium.

Cooperrider, D.L. & Godwin, L.N. (2012). Positive organization development: Innovation-inspired change in an economy and ecology of strengths. In K.S. Cameron, & G.M. Spreitzer, (Eds.) The *Oxford handbook of positive organizational scholarship.* (pp. 737-750). New York: Oxford University Press.

Cooperrider, D.L. & Sekerka, L. (2003). Toward a theory of positive organizational change In K. Cameron, J. Dutton, & R. Quinn, (Eds.). *Positive organizational scholarship.* (pp. 225-240). San Francisco: Berrett-Koehler.

Cory, D. (1998). The killing fields: Institutions and the death of our spirits. In L.C.Spears, (Ed.). *Insights on leadership: Service, stewardship, spirit, and servant-leadership.* (pp. 209–215). *New* York: John Wiley & Sons, Inc.

Duncan, T. (2012). Glimpses of wonder. Living with disagreement. *Retrieved from http:// metanexus.net/blog/living-disagreement?utm_source=2012*

Eisen, S. (2010). The personhood of the OD practitioner. In W.J. Rothwell, J.M. Stavros, R. Sullivan & A. Sullivan (Eds.). *Practicing Organization Development: A guide for leading change.* (pp. 527-545). San Francisco, CA: John Wiley and Sons, Inc.

Gergen, K.J. (1994). *Realities and relationships: Soundings in social construction.* Cambridge: Harvard University Press.

Gergen, K.J. (2009). *Relational being: Beyond self and community.* Oxford: Oxford University Press.

Gergen, M. M. (2001). *Feminist reconstructions in psychology: Narrative, gender and performance.* Thousand Oaks: CA: Sage Publications.

Hartnett, T. (2011). *The basics of consensus decision-making.* Gabriola Island, BC, Canada: New Society Publishers.

Henriques, J. (1984). Social psychology and the politics of racism. In H. Henriques, W. Hollway, C. Urwin, C. Venn, & V. Walkerdine, *Changing the subject: Psychology, social regulation and subjectivity.* (pp. 60-89). London: Merhuen

Herrera-Viedma, e., Herrera, F, & Chiclana, F. (2002). A consensus model for multiperson decision making with different preference structures. *IEE Transactions on Systems, Man and Cybernetics—Part A: Systems and Humans, Vol 32, No. 3.*

Hosking & McNamee (2011). *Research and social change: A relational constructionist approach.* London: Routledge.

Hosking, D.M. & Pluut, B. (2010). (Re)constructing reflexivity: A relational constructionist approach. *The qualitative report.* Volume 15 Number 1 January 2010, 59-75.

Huebner, D.E. (1999). Spirituality and knowing. In V. Hillis (Ed.), *The lure of the transcendent: Collected essays by Dwayne E. Huebner* (pp. 353-378). Mahwah, NJ: Erlbaum.

Isaacs, W. (1999). *Dialogue and the art of thinking together: A pioneering approach to communicating in business and in life.* New York: Doubleday.

Jaques, E. (1990). In praise of hierarchy. *Harvard Business Review 68 (1),* 127 – 133.

Kark, R. (2012). Workplace intimacy in leader-follower relationships. In K.S. Cameron, & G.M. Spreitzer, (Eds.) The *Oxford handbook of positive organizational scholarship.* (pp. 423-438). New York: Oxford University Press.

Katz, D. & Kahn, R.L. (2005). Organizations and the system concept. In *Classics of organization theory.* pp. 480-490. Belmont, CA: Thomson Wadsworth.

Mahaffy, S. (2012). *Relational presence: The spatiality of breakthrough decision making through a relational-constructionist lens.* Unpublished dissertation. Taos Institute/Tilburg University.

McNamee, S. & Gergen, K. (1999). *Relational responsibility: Resources for sustainable dialogue.* Thousand Oaks, CA: Sage Publications.

Mirvis, P.H. (2010). Transformational learning journeys: Seeing is believing. In W.J. Rothwell, J.M. Stavros, R. Sullivan, & A. Sullivan (Eds.). *Practicing Organization Development: A guide for leading change.* (pp. 516-526). San Francisco, CA: John Wiley and Sons, Inc.

Nguyen Huy, Q. (2012). Emotions and strategic change. In K.S. Cameron, & G.M. Spreitzer, (Eds.) *The Oxford handbook of positive organizational scholarship.* (pp. 811-824). New York: Oxford University Press.

Nielsen, R.P. (1998). Quaker foundations for Greenleaf's servant-leadership and "friendly disentangling" method. In L.C. Spears (Ed.). *Insights on leadership: Service, stewardship, spirit, and servant-leadership.* (pp. 126–144). New York: John Wiley & Sons, Inc.

Pfeffer, J. (2005). Understanding the role of power in decision making. In J.M. Schafritz, J.S. Ott, Suk Jang, Yong. (Eds.). *Classics of organization theory.* (pp. 2893-303). Belmont, CA: Thomson Wadsworth.

Polak, F. (1973). *The image of the future.* E. Boulding, Trans. Amsterdam: Elsevier Scientific Publishing Company.

Rhizome (2011). A brief history of consensus decision making. *Retrieved Oct. 2012 from* http://rhizomenetwork.wordpress.com/tag/quakers/

Rinderknecht, D. (2004). *Integral Pedagogy: Teaching with an open and engaged heart.* Retrieved from UMI Dissertation Services (UMI Number 3158594). Ann Arbor, MI.

Schön, D. (1983). *The reflective practitioner: How professionals think in action.* New York:

Basic Books.

Senge, P., Kleiner, A., Roberts, C., Ross, R., Roth, G., Smith, B. (1999). *The dance of change: The challenges of sustaining momentum in learning organizations: A fifth discipline resource.* New York: Doubleday.

Senge, P., Scharmer, C.O., Jaworski, J., & Flowers, B.S. (2004*). Presence: Human purpose and the field of the future.* Cambridge, MA: Society for Organizational Learning.

Sheeran, M.J. (1996). *Beyond majority rule: Voteless decisions in the Religious Society of Friends.* Philadelphia: Philadelphia Yearly Meeting, Religious Society of Friends.

Simmel, G. (1972). *On individuality and social forms.* (D. Levine, Ed. and Trans.). Chicago: University of Chicago Press.

Spreitzer, G.M. & Cameron, K.C. (2012). A path forward: Assessing progress and exploring core questions for the future of positive organizational scholarship In K.S. Cameron, & G.M. Spreitzer, (Eds.) The *Oxford handbook of positive organizational scholarship.* (pp. 1034-1048). New York: Oxford University Press.

Stavros, J.M. & Torres, C. (2008). Dynamic *Relationships: Unleashing the power of appreciative inquiry in daily living.* Chagrin Falls, OH: Taos Institute Publications.

Stavros, J.M. & Wooten, L. (2012). Positive strategy: Creating and sustaining strengths-based strategy that SOARs and performs. In K.S. Cameron, & G.M. Spreitzer, (Eds.) The *Oxford handbook of positive organizational scholarship.* (pp. 825-839). New York: Oxford University Press.

Urwin, C. (1984). Power relations and the emergence of language. In H. Henriques, W. Hollway, C. Urwin, C. Venn, & V. Walkerdine, *Changing the subject: Psychology, social regulation and subjectivity.* (pp. 264-322). London: Merhuen.

Watkins, J.M. (2010). The shifting field of OD practice. In W.J. Rothwell, J.M. Stavros, R. Sullivan, & A. Sullivan (Eds.). *Practicing Organization Development: A guide for leading change.* (pp. 634-638). San Francisco, CA: John Wiley and Sons, Inc.

Watkins, J.M. & Stavros, J.M. (2010). Appreciative inquiry: OD in the post-modern age. In W.J. Rothwell, J.M. Stavros, R.L. Sullivan, A. Sullivan, (Eds.). *Practicing organization development: A guide for leading change.* (pp. 158-181). San Francisco: John

Watsuji, T., (1992), *Watsuji Tetsurô Zenshû: Complete Works of Watsuji Tetsurô, 27 vols.*, Abe Yoshishigo et al (Eds.), Tokyo: Iwanami Shoten.

Weiss, A. (2003). *Organizational consulting: How to be an effective internal change agent.* Hoboken, NJ: John Wiley & Sons, Inc.

Zukav, G. (1996). Conversation with Gary Zukav. In *Towards a new world view: Conversations at the leading edge with Russell DiCarlo.* Erie, PA: Epic Publishing.

www.ingramcontent.com/pod-product-compliance
Lightning Source LLC
Chambersburg PA
CBHW081244180526
45171CB00005B/535